For Tamara, Ashley and Jody, with love – V.B.
To Cherry and Sophie – D.A.

Some words you may not know –
A **guinep** is a small fruit which can be popped into your mouth once you have cracked open the outer shell.
A **jackfruit** is a large, oval fruit. Inside the spiky green skin there are cream-coloured, chewy pods each containing a cream-coloured seed.
A **jew-plum** is the size of a small pear. It has sweet tangy flesh over a spiky stone.
A **naseberry** is brown and the size of a large egg. It has very sweet brown flesh and dark brown seeds.
The **red apples** in the text are Caribbean Otaheiti apples. They are pear shaped and very sweet and juicy.
Smaddy means "somebody".
A **sweet-sop** is a very sweet fruit, which has a rough outside and a white inside with black stones.

'Fruits' is taken from *Duppy Jamboree*,
first published by Cambridge University Press in 1992.
This edition first published 1997 by Macmillan Children's Books,
a division of Macmillan Publishers Limited,
25 Eccleston Place, London SW1W 9NF and Basingstoke.
Associated companies worldwide.
Text copyright © 1992 Valerie Bloom
Illustrations copyright © 1997 David Axtell
The right of Valerie Bloom and David Axtell to be identified as the author and
illustrator of this work has been asserted by them in accordance with
the Copyright, Design and Patents Act 1988.
ISBN (HB) 0 333 65311 4
3 5 7 9 8 6 4 2

ISBN (PB) 0 333 65312 2
3 5 7 9 8 6 4

A CIP catalogue record for this book is available from the British Library.
Printed in Hong Kong.

FRUITS

a Caribbean counting poem

by Valerie Bloom

Illustrated by David Axtell

MACMILLAN CHILDREN'S BOOKS

Half a pawpaw in the basket –
Only one o' we can have it.
Wonder which one that will be?
I have a feeling that is me.

One guinep up in the tree

Hanging down there tempting me.

It don' mek no sense to pick it,

One guinep can't feed a cricket.

Two ripe guava pon the shelf,

I know I hide them there meself.

When night come an' it get dark

Me an' them will have a talk.

Three sweet-sop, well I jus' might

Give one o' them a nice big bite.

Cover up the bite jus' so, sis,

Then no one will ever notice.

Four red apple near me chair –

Who so careless put them there?

Them don' know how me love apple?

Well, thank God fe silly people.

Five jew-plum, I can't believe it!

How they know jew-plum's me fav'rit?

But why they hide them in the cupboard?

Cho, people can be so awkward.

Six naseberry, you want a nibble?

Why baby must always dribble?

Come wipe you mout', it don't mek sense

To broadcast the evidence.

Seven mango! What a find!

The smaddy who lef them really kind.

One fe you an' six fe me,

If you want more, climb the tree.

Eight orange fe cousin Clem,

But I have just one problem –

How to get rid o' the eight skin

That the orange them come in.

Nine jackfruit! Not even me

Can finish nine, but let me see,

I don't suppose that they will miss one.

That was hard, but now me done.

Ten banana, mek them stay,

I feeling really full today.

Mek me lie down on me bed, quick.

Lawd, ah feeling really sick.

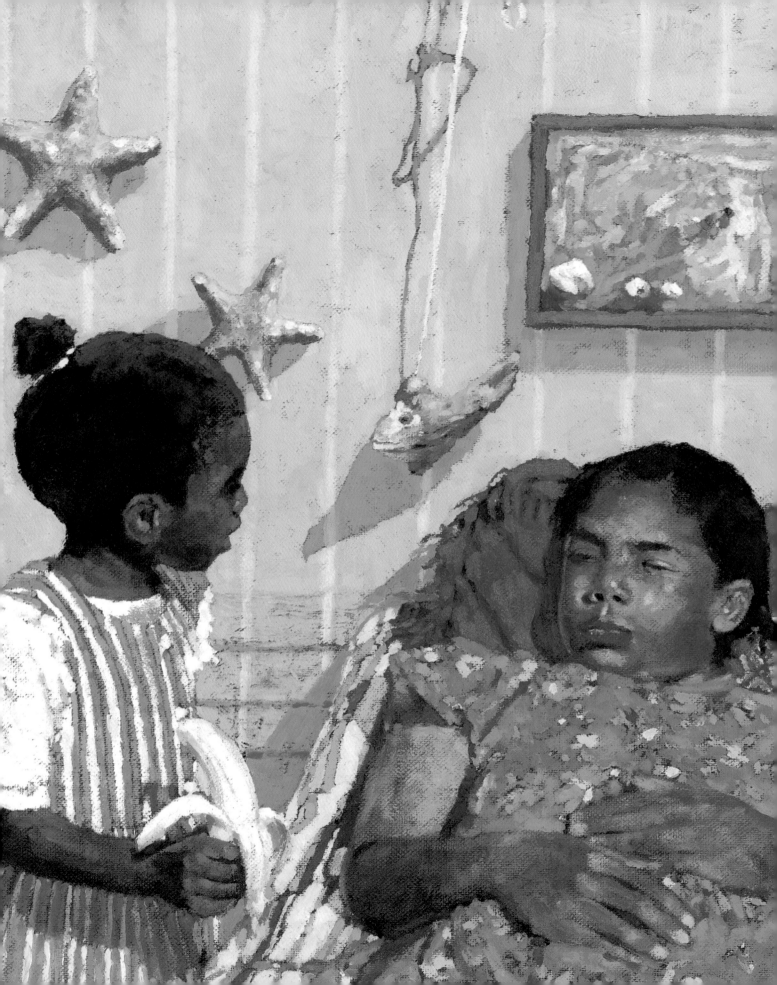